Interior Design Coloring Book For Adults

PLEASE ROTATE THE BOOK. THE COLORING PAGES ARE PRINTED HORIZONTALLY.

HAPPY COLORING!

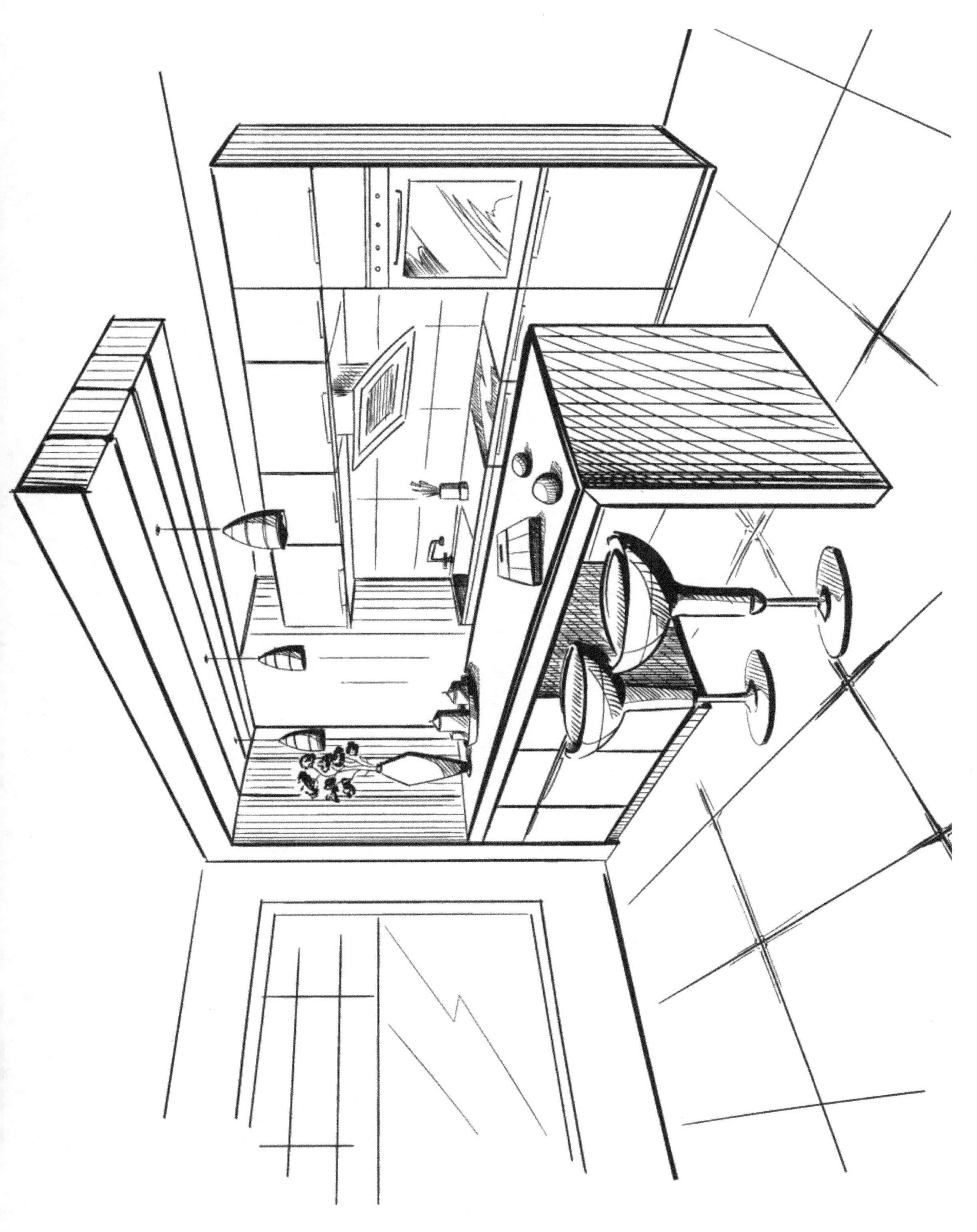

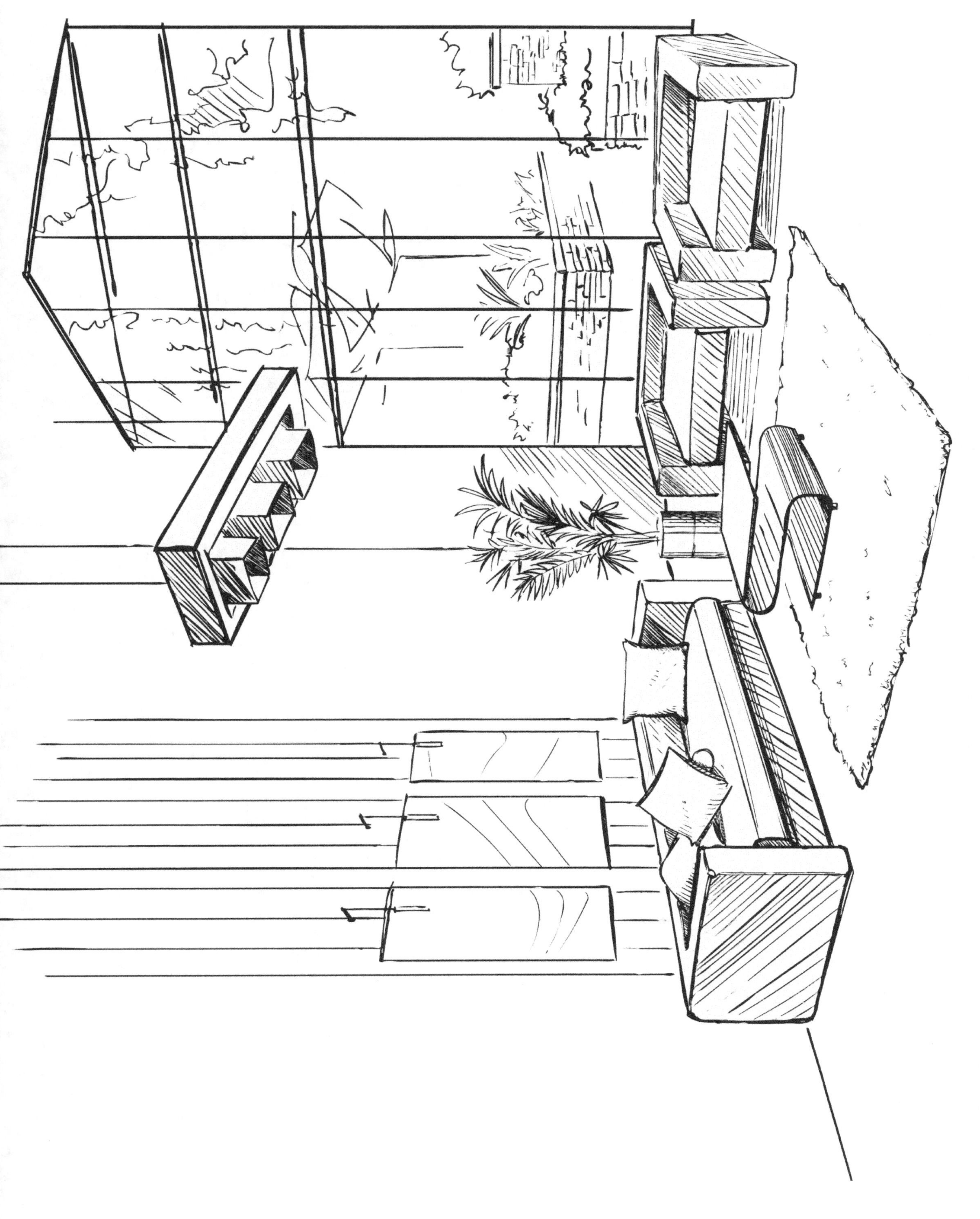

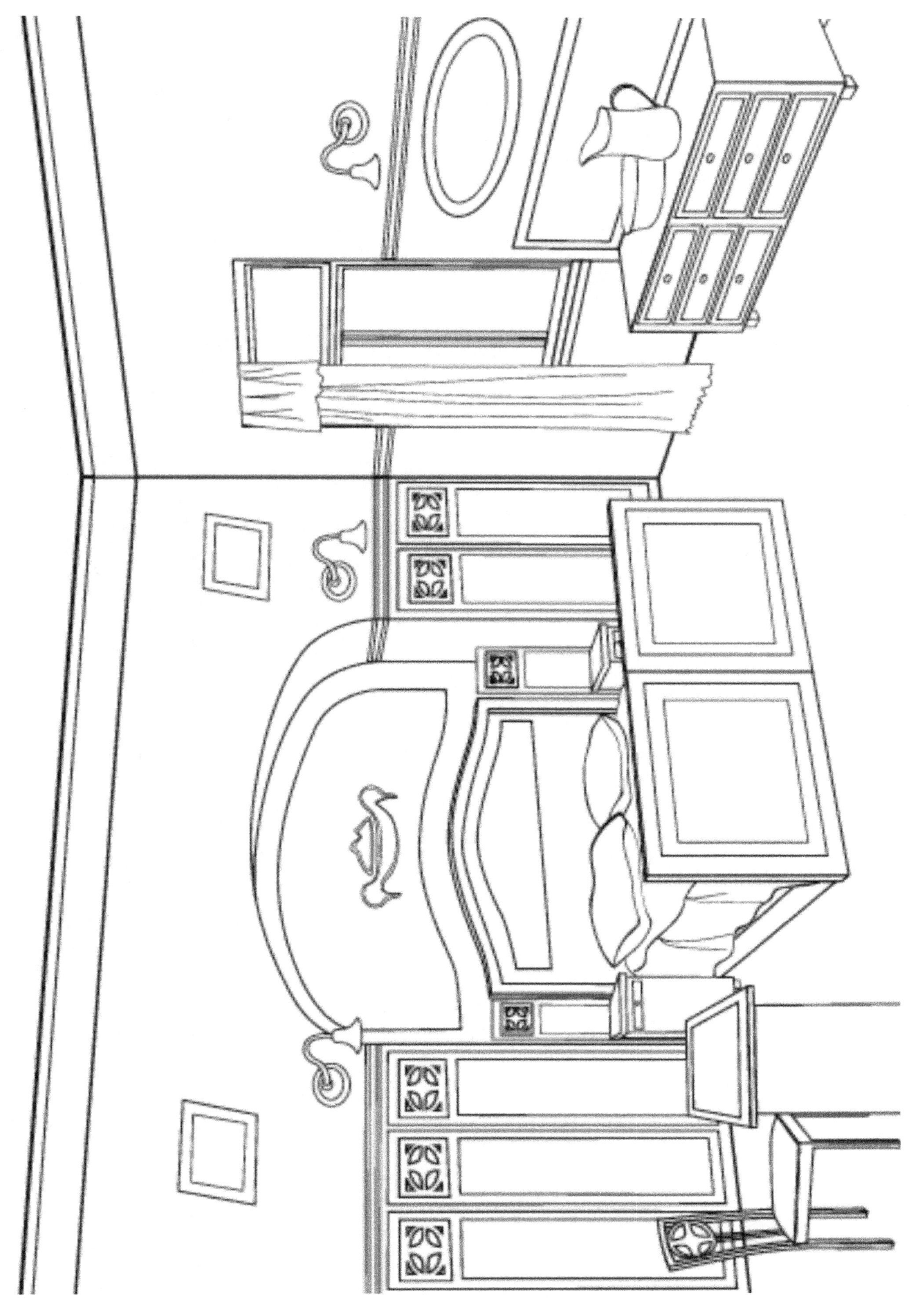

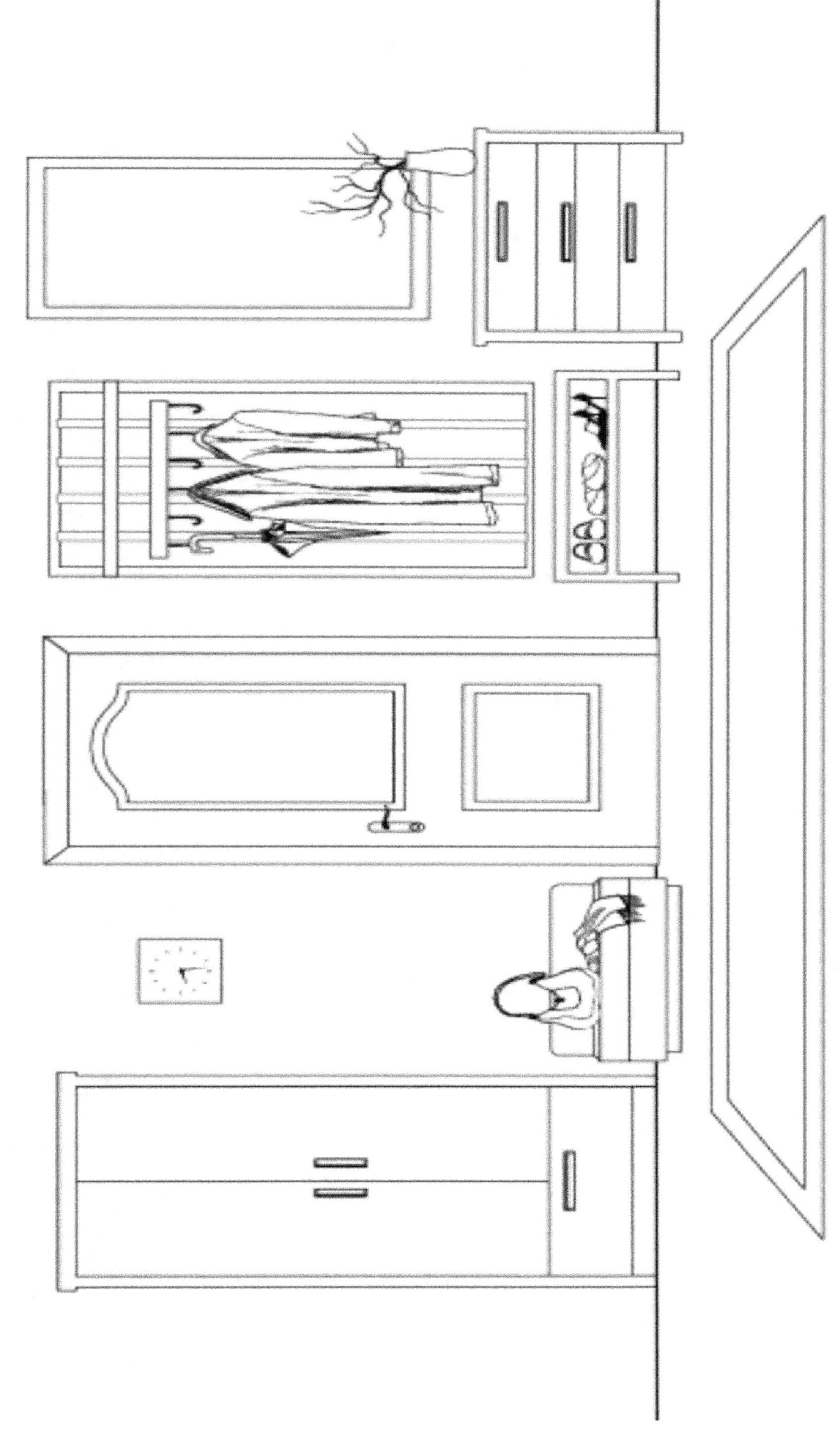

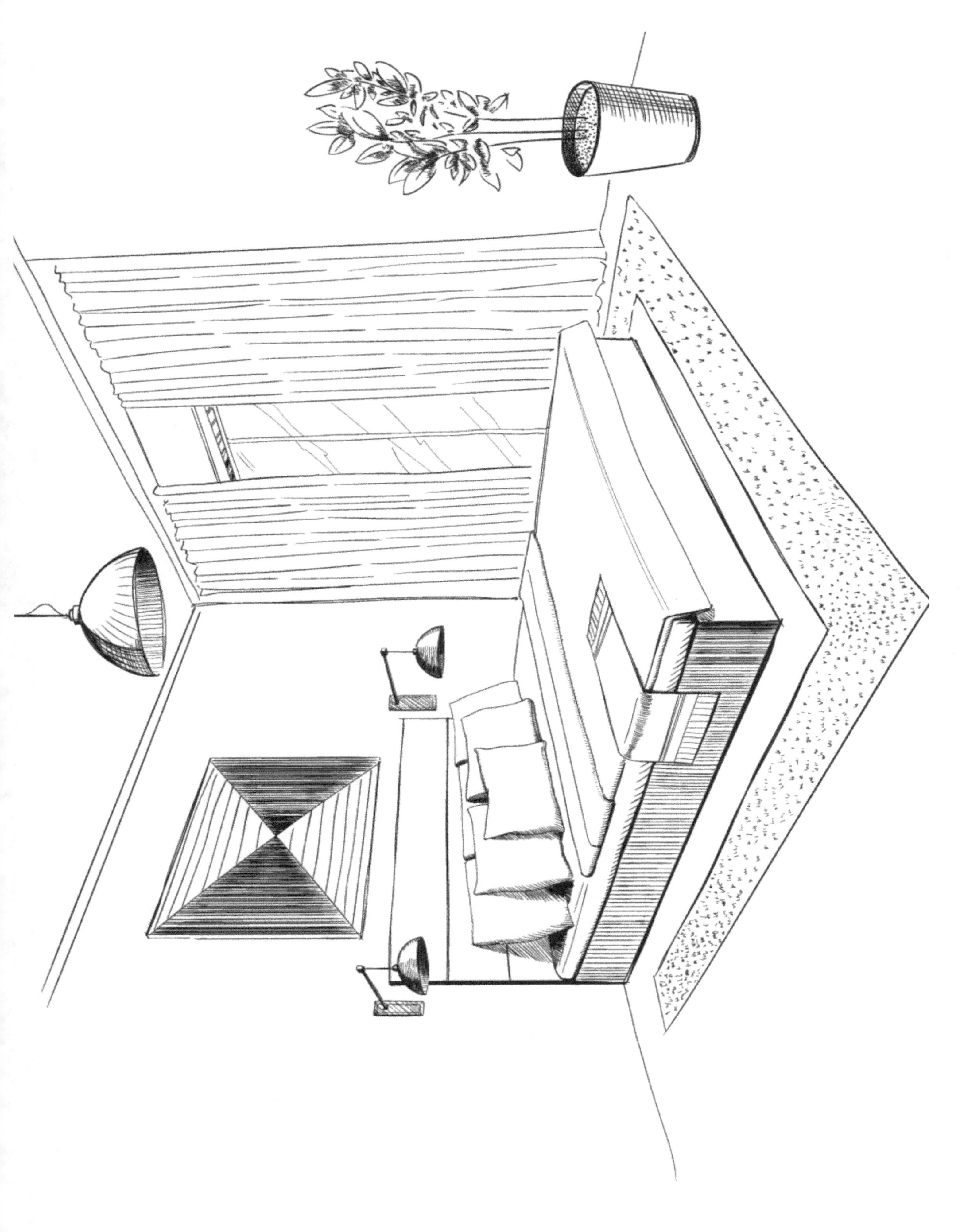

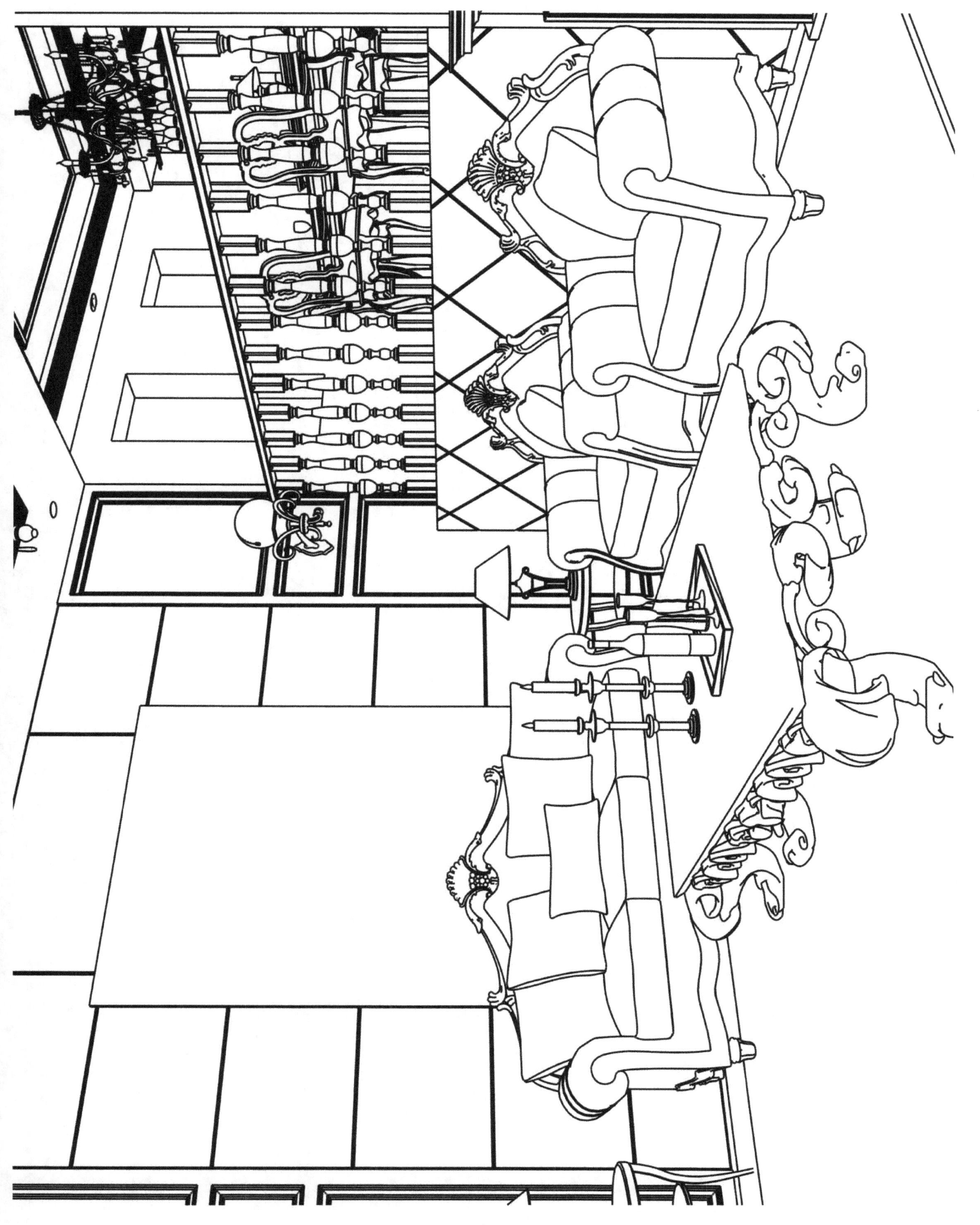

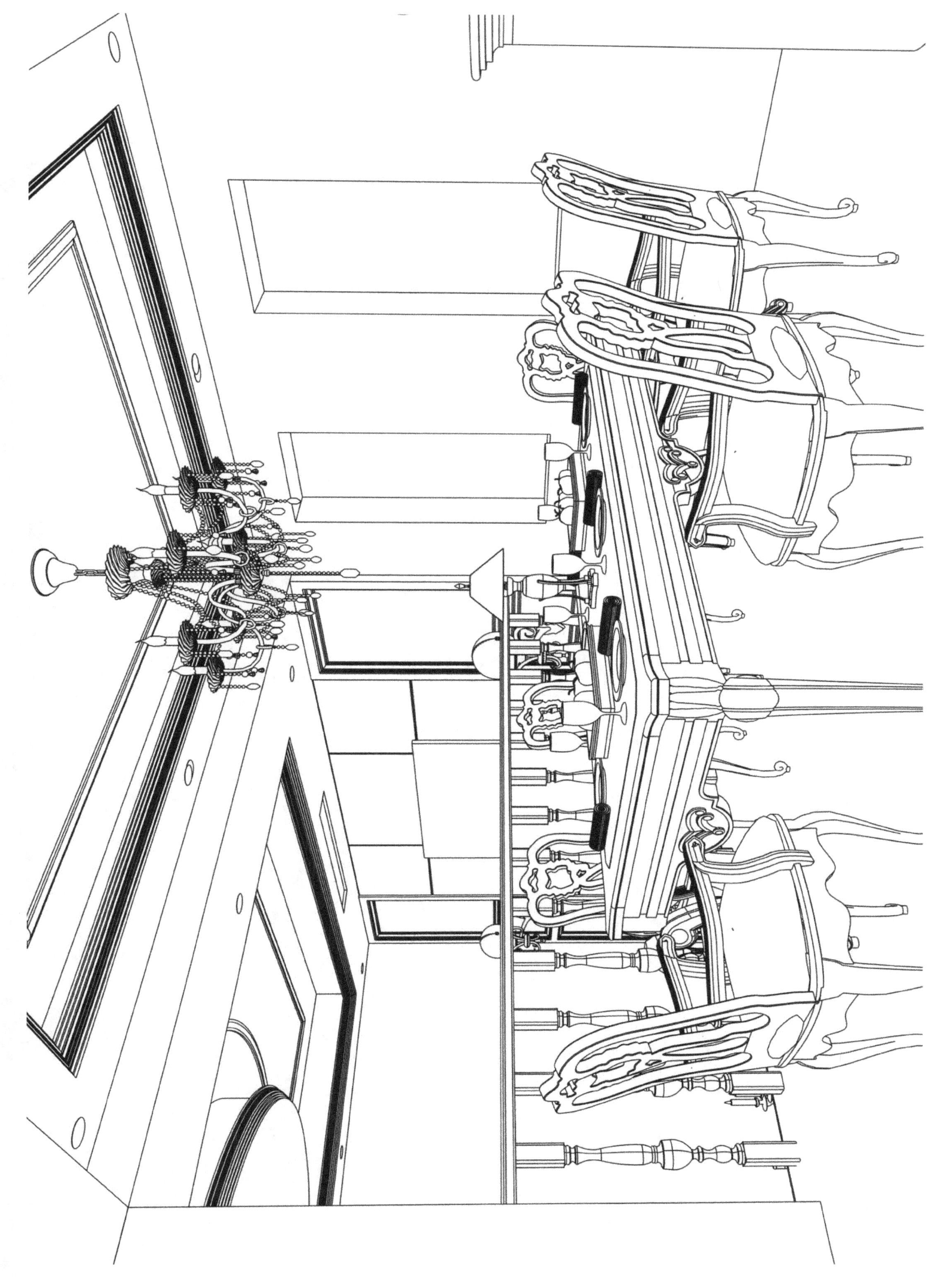

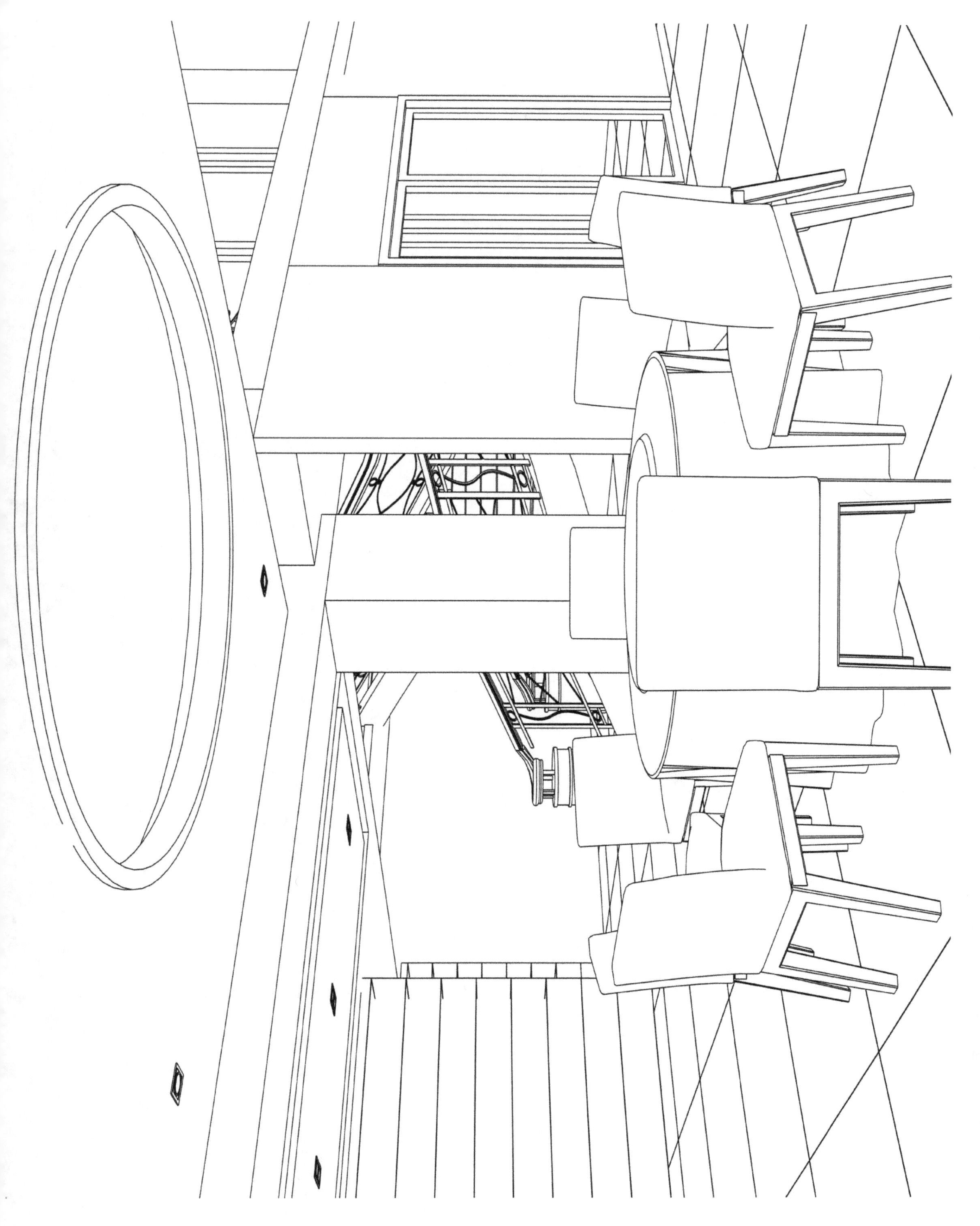

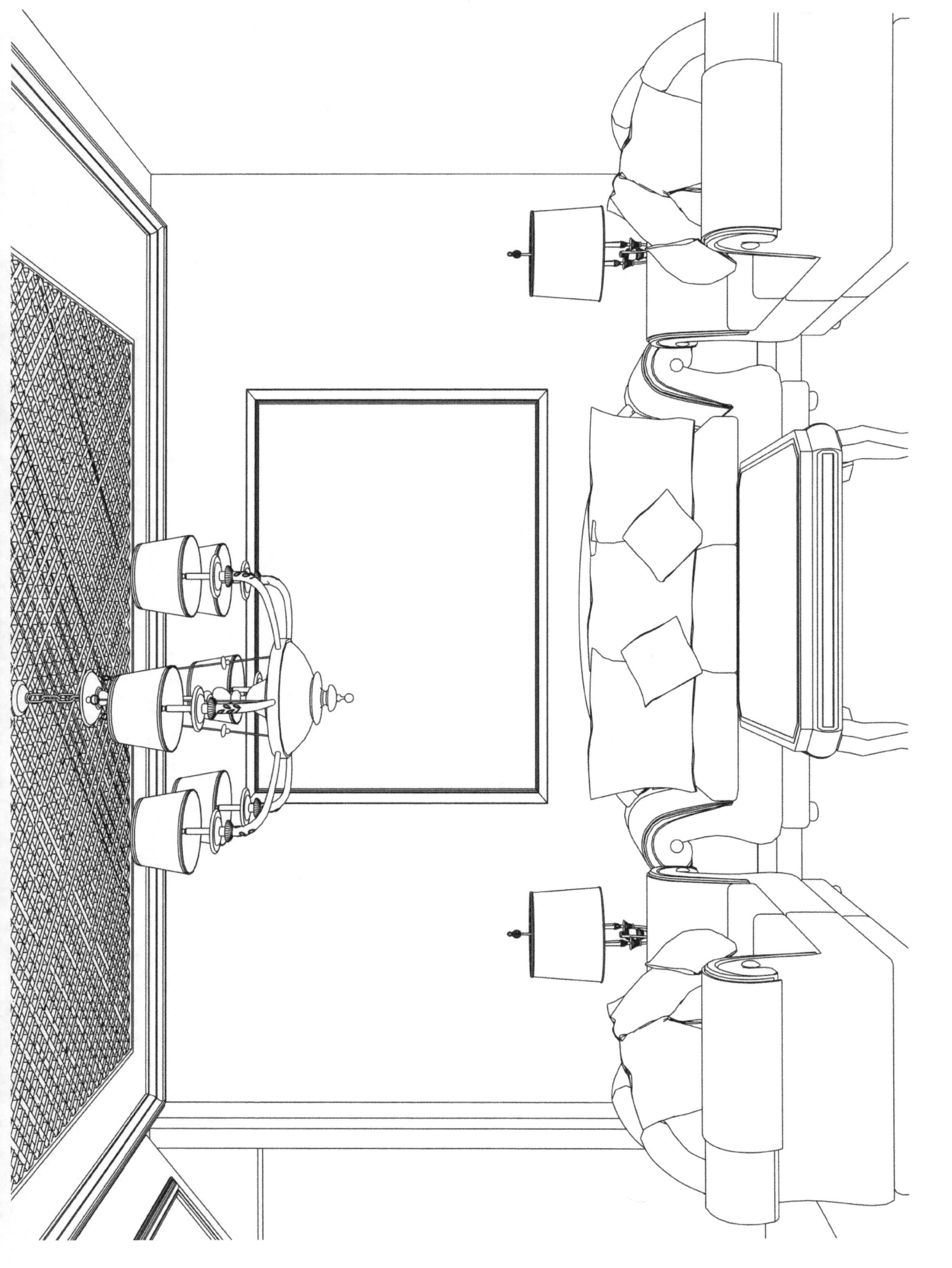

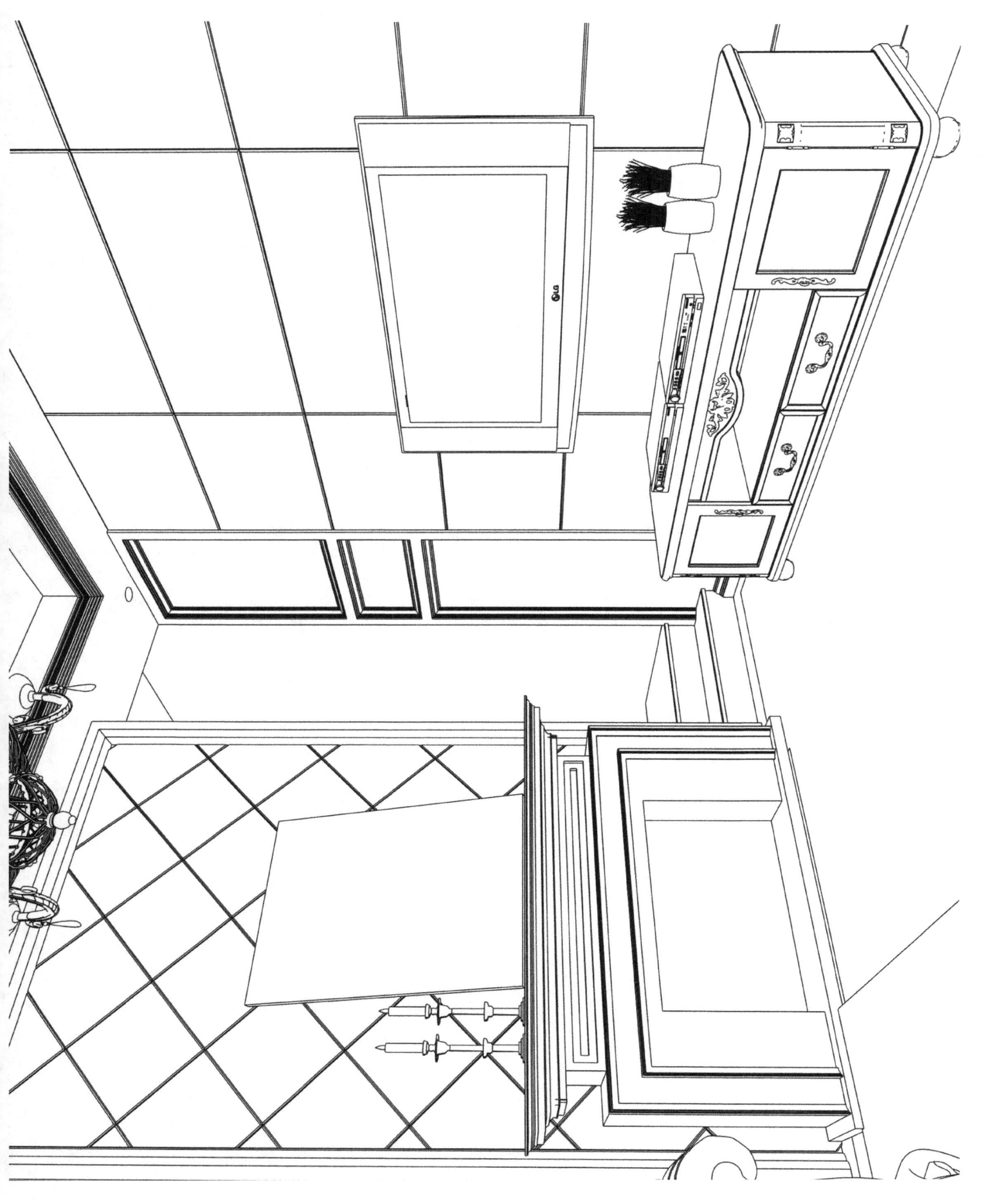

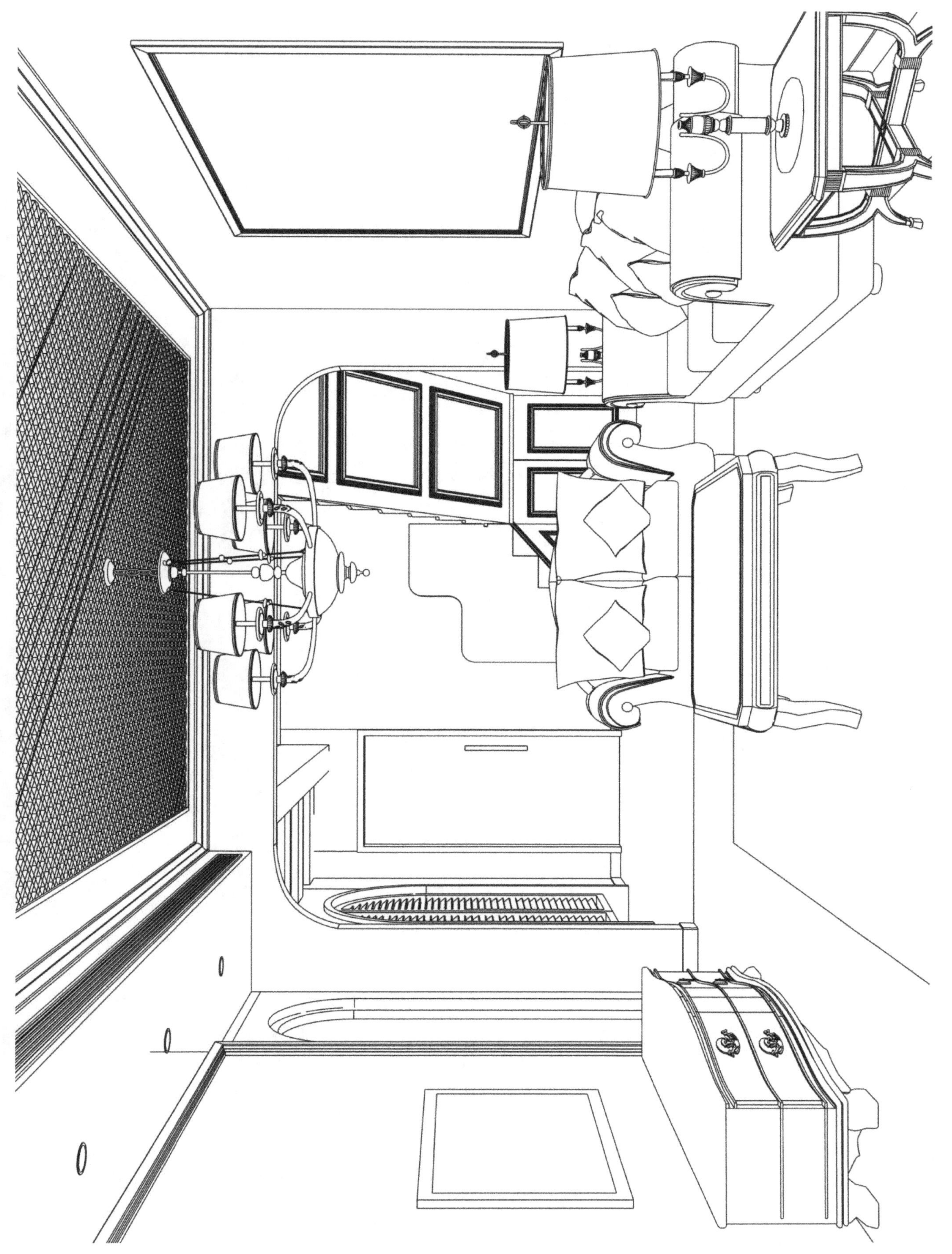

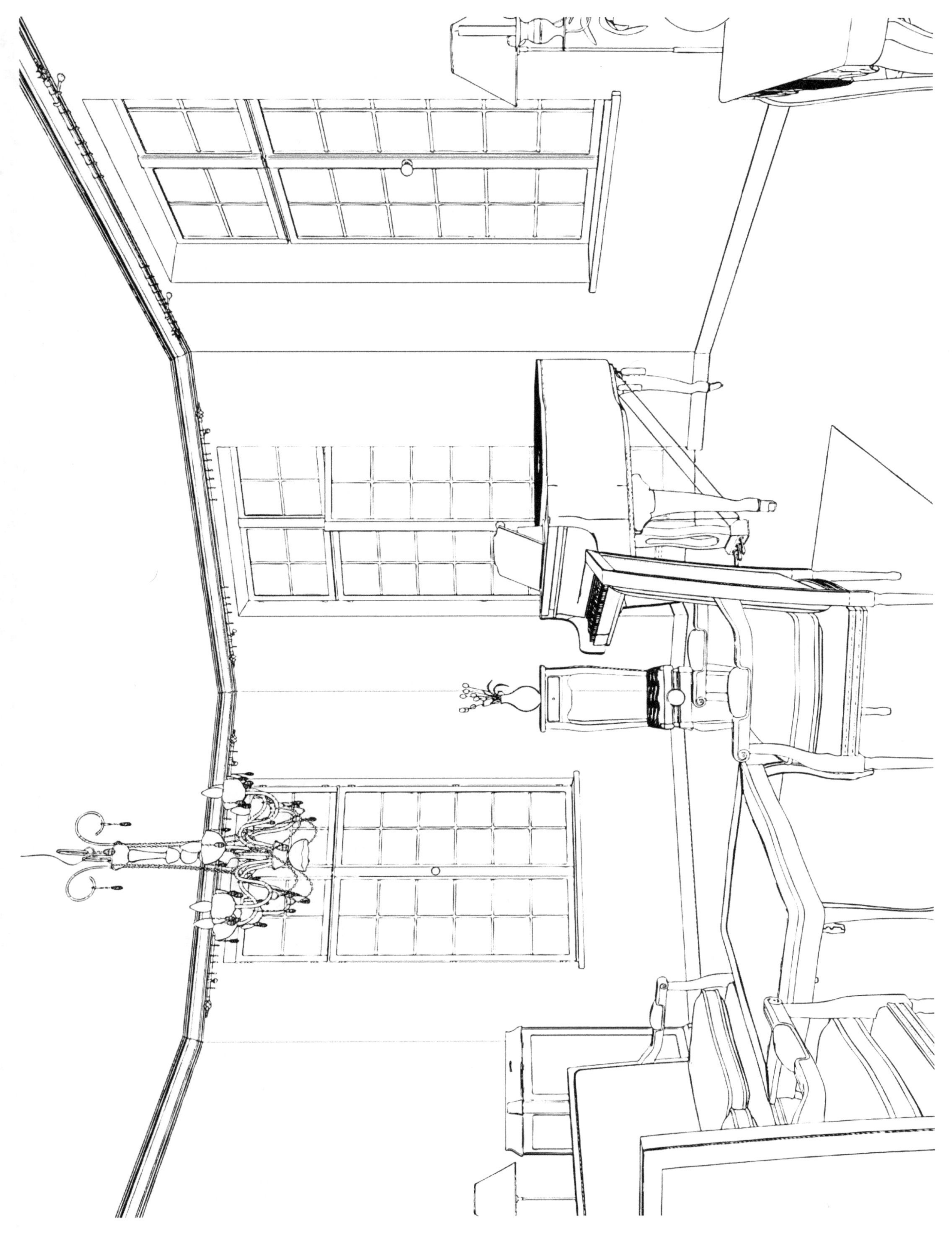

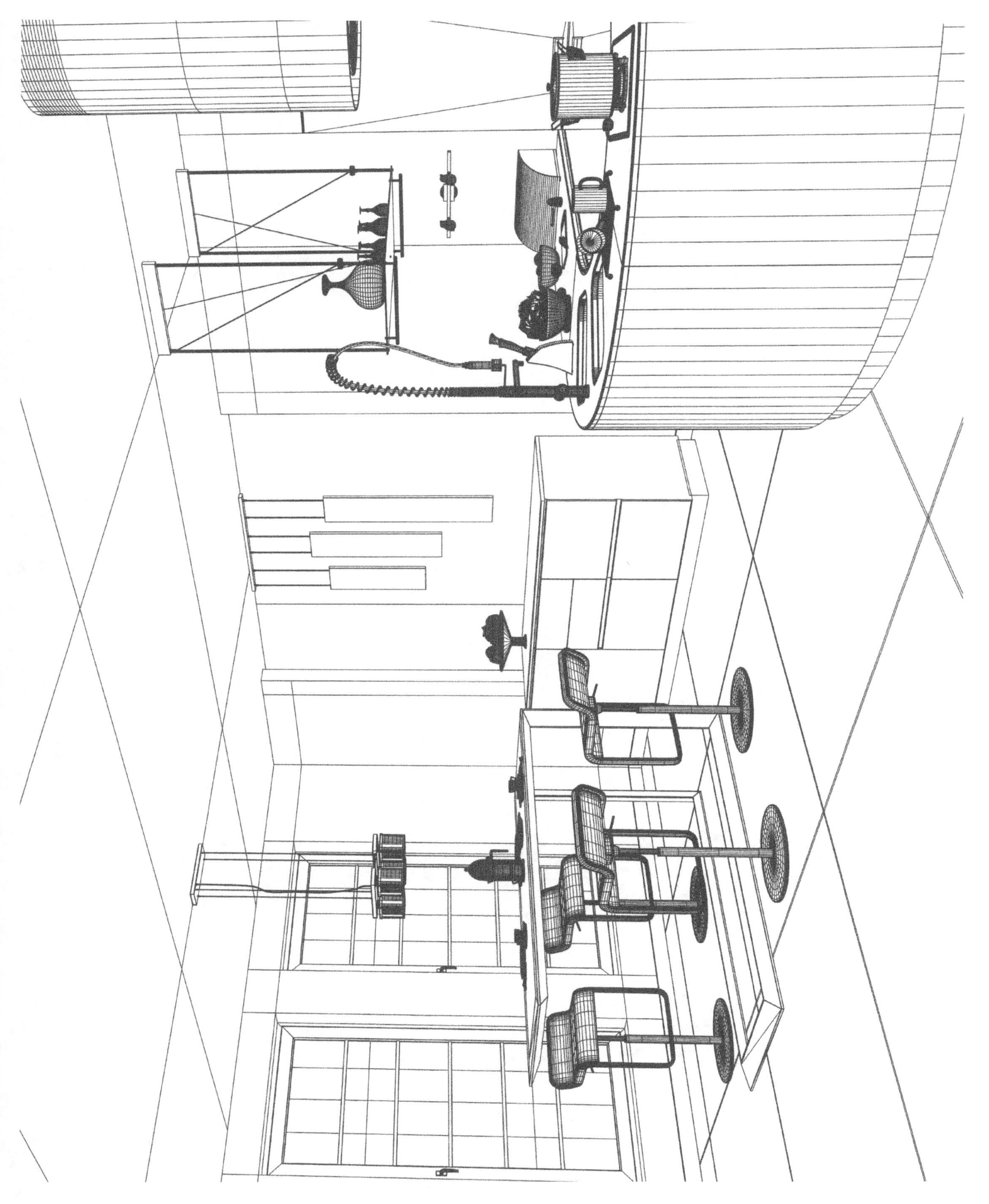

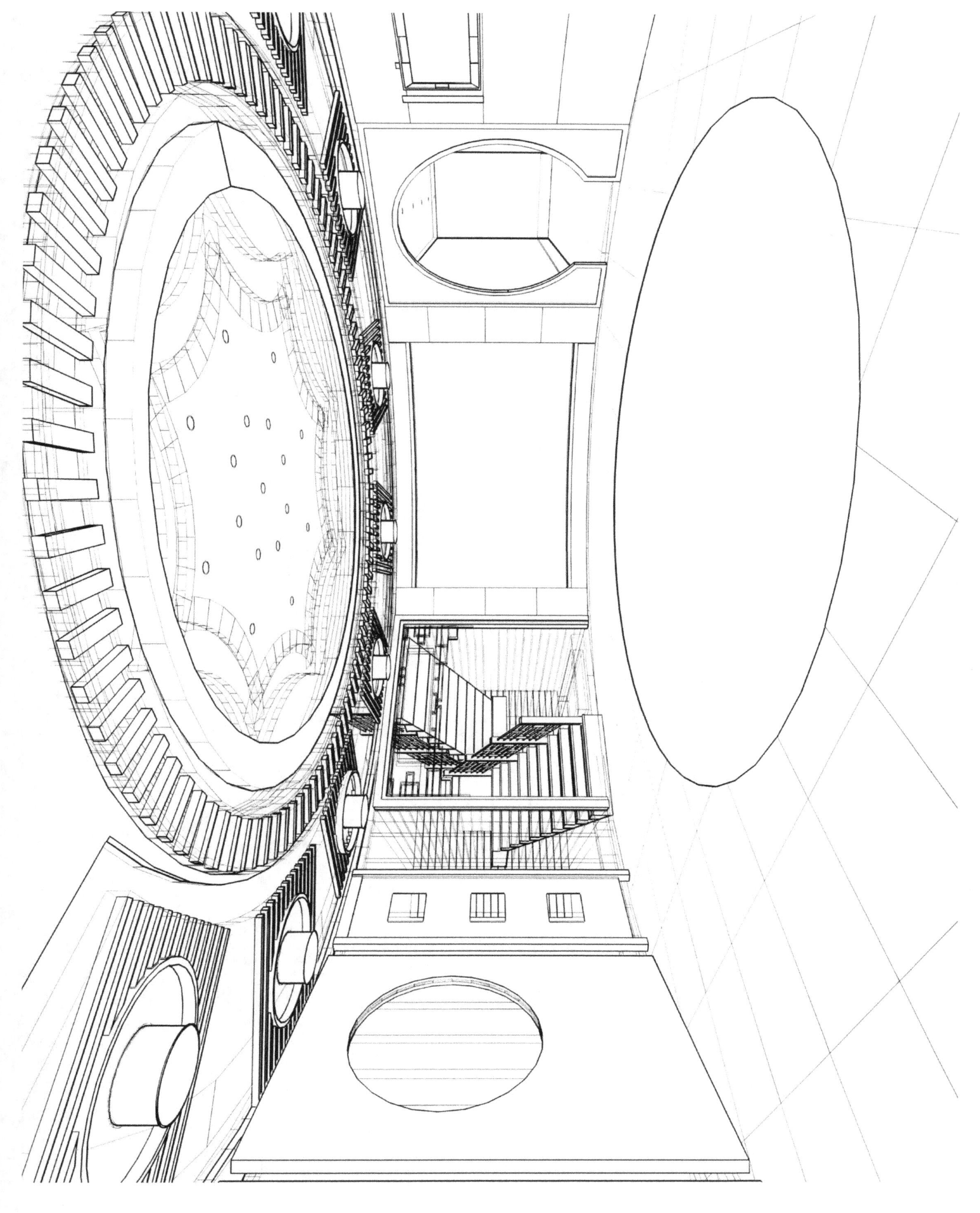

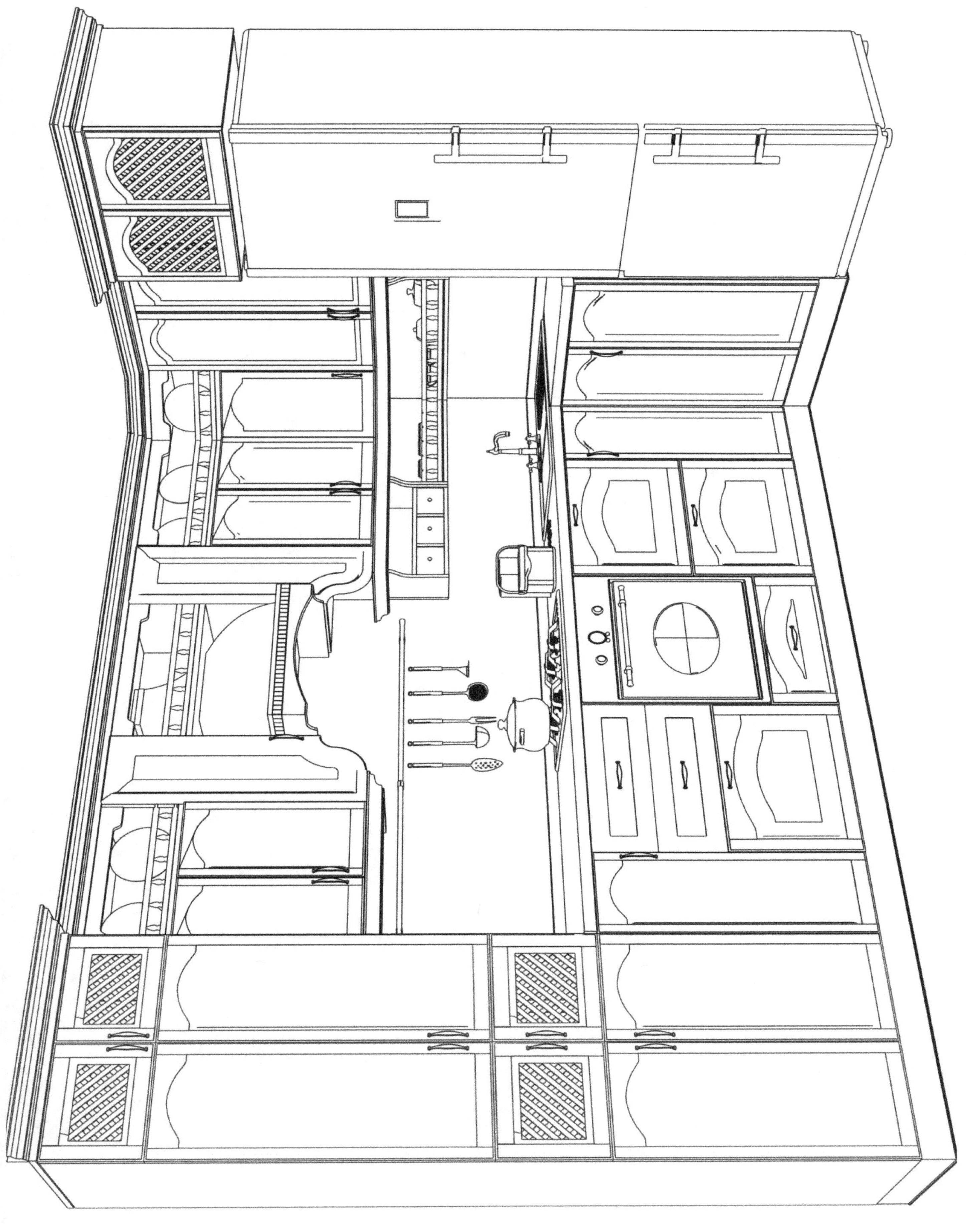

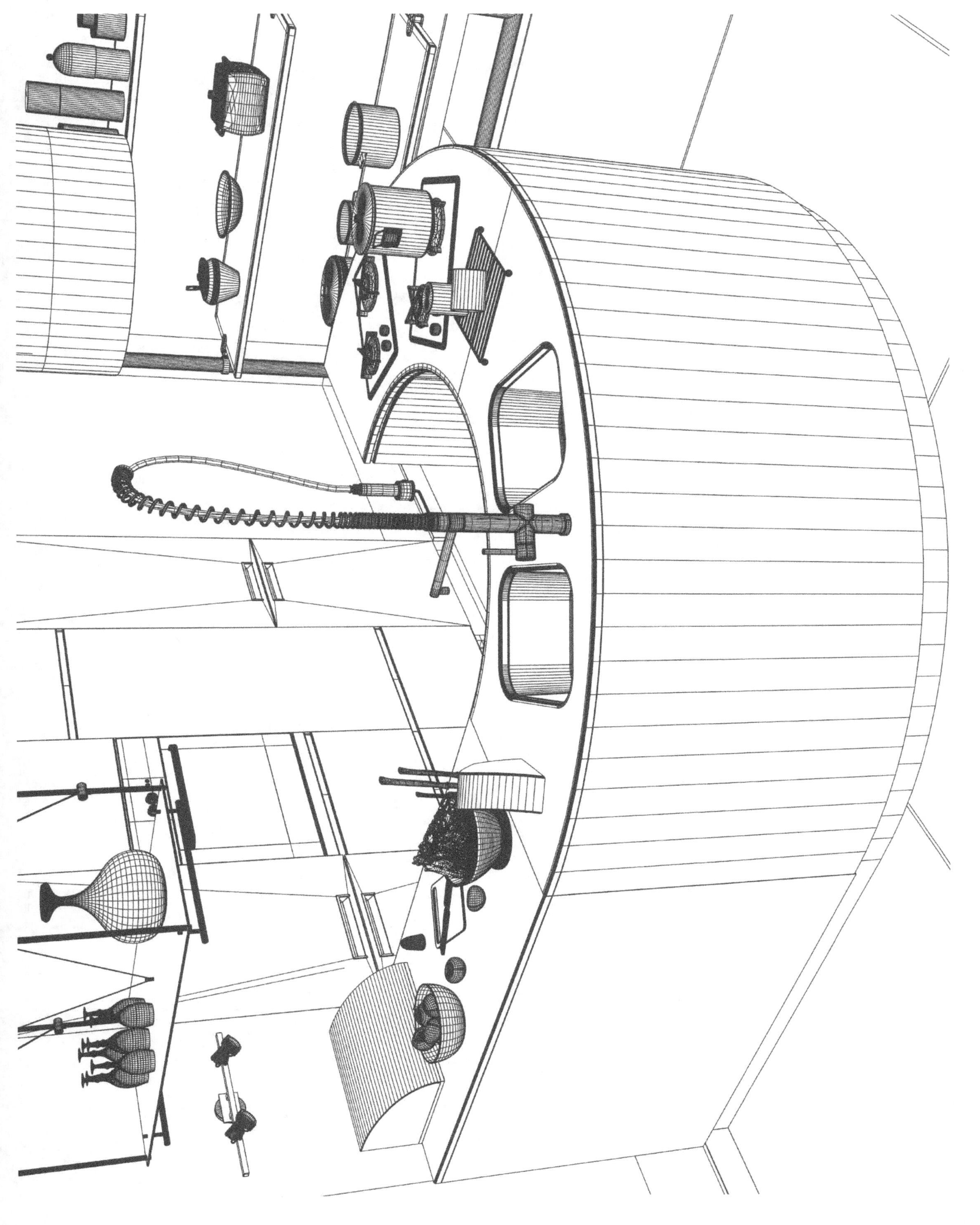

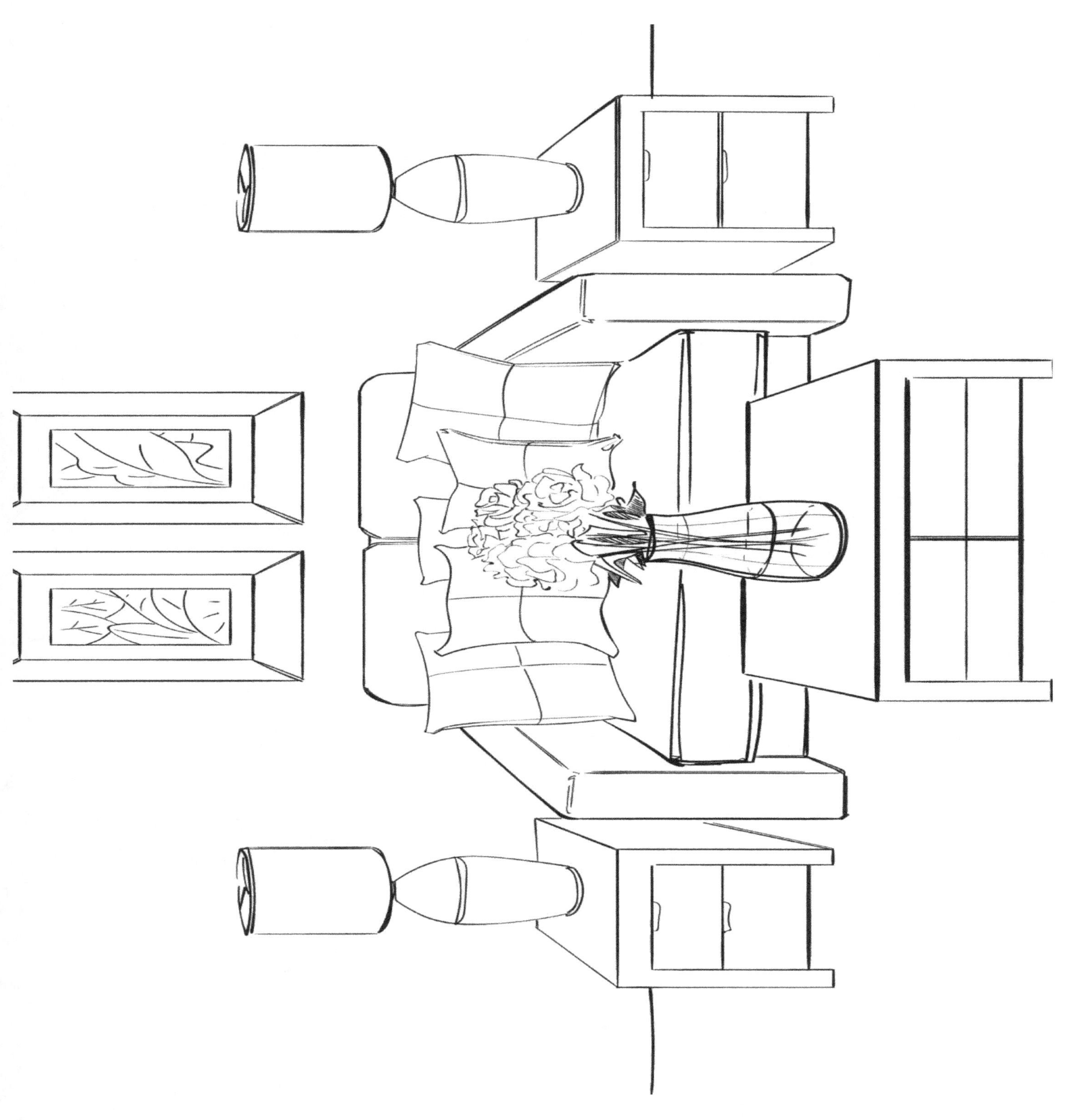

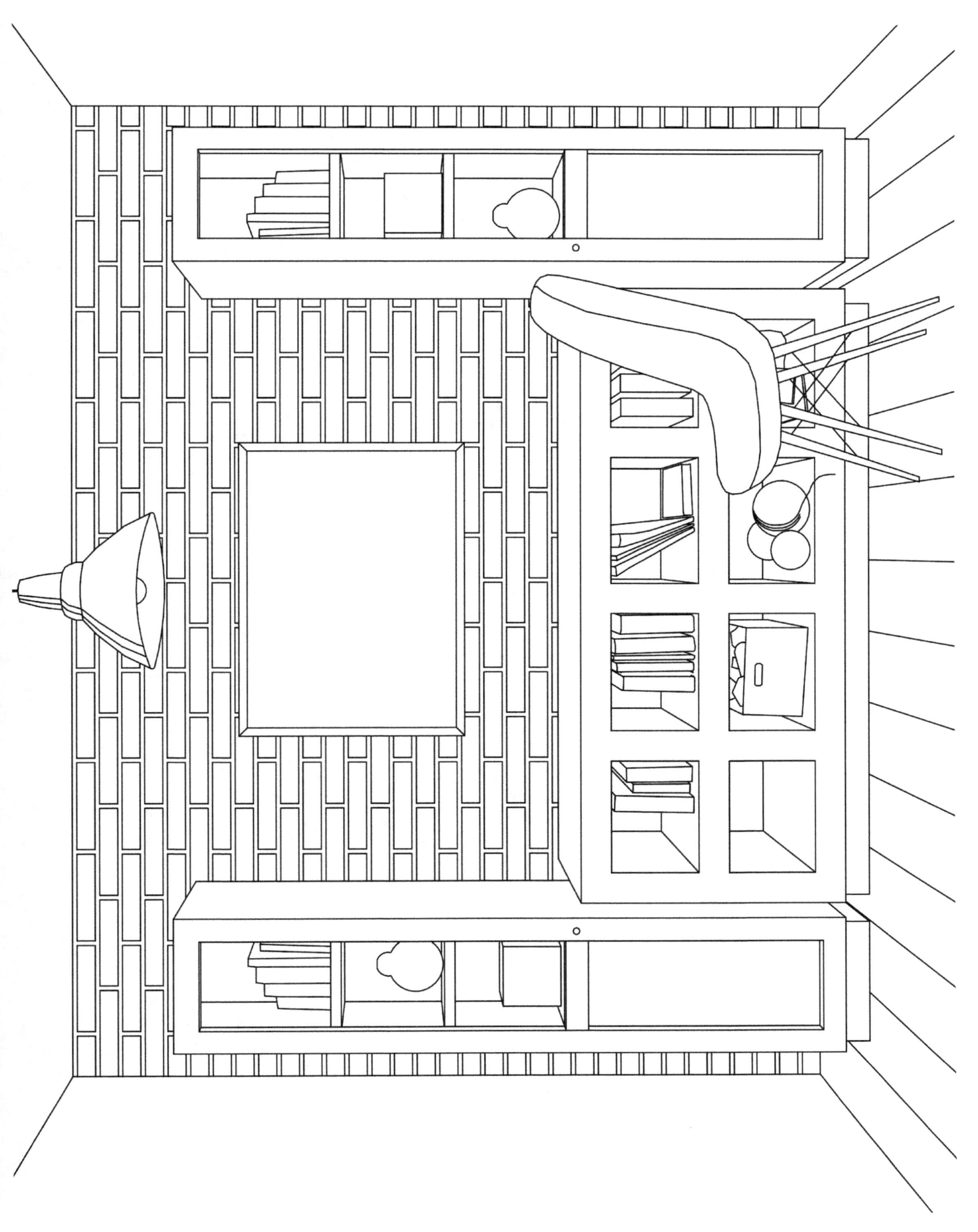

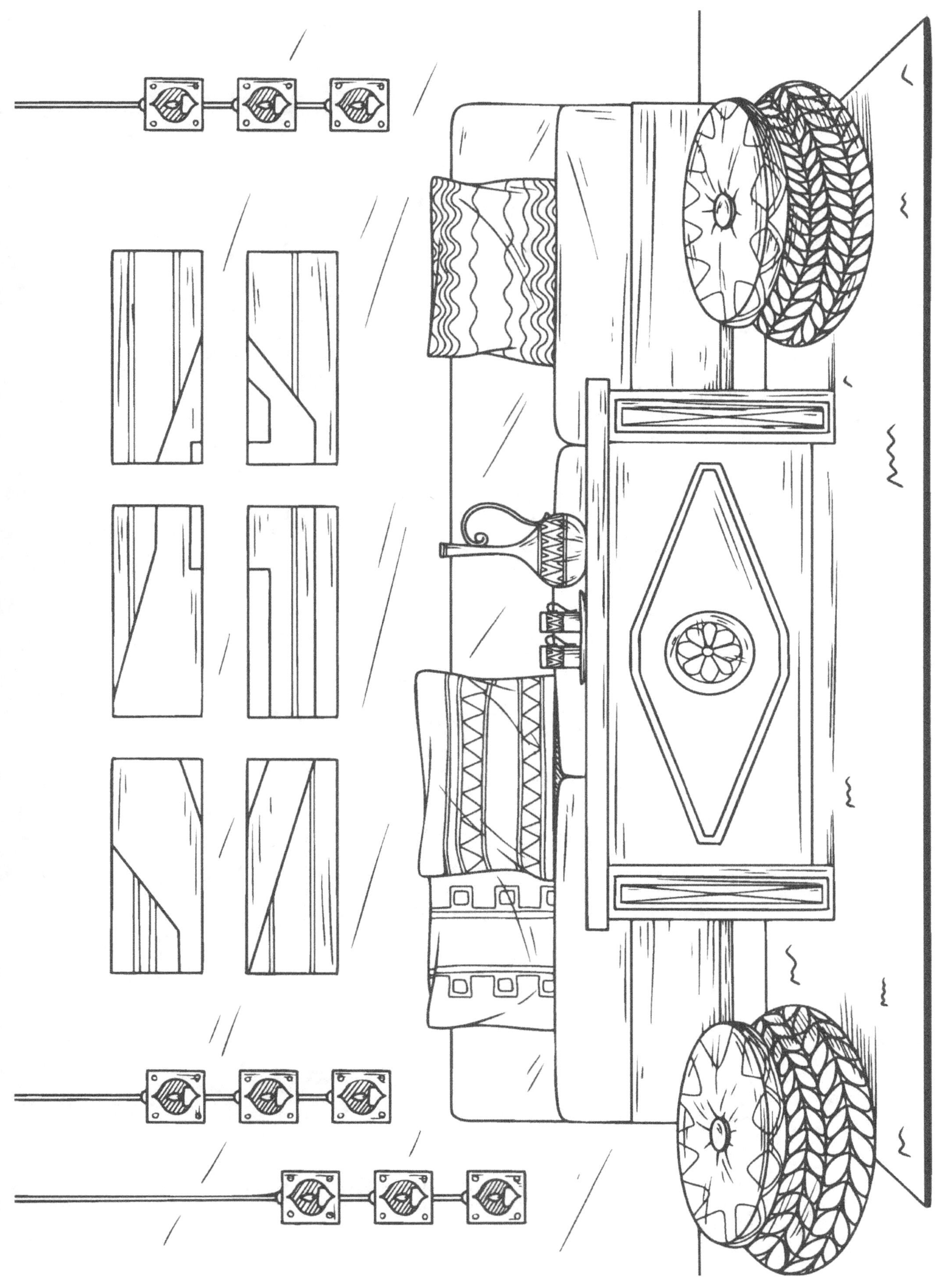

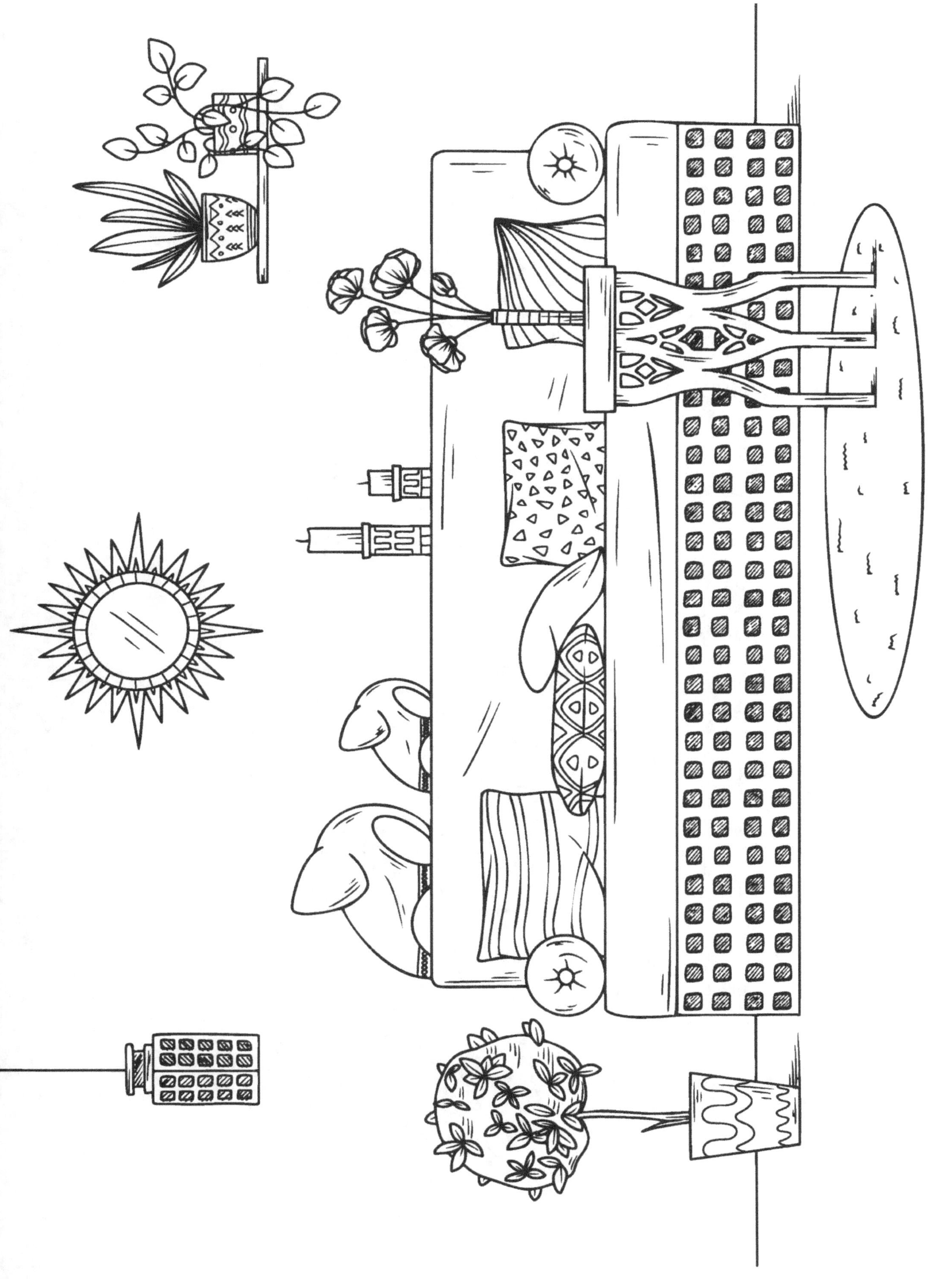

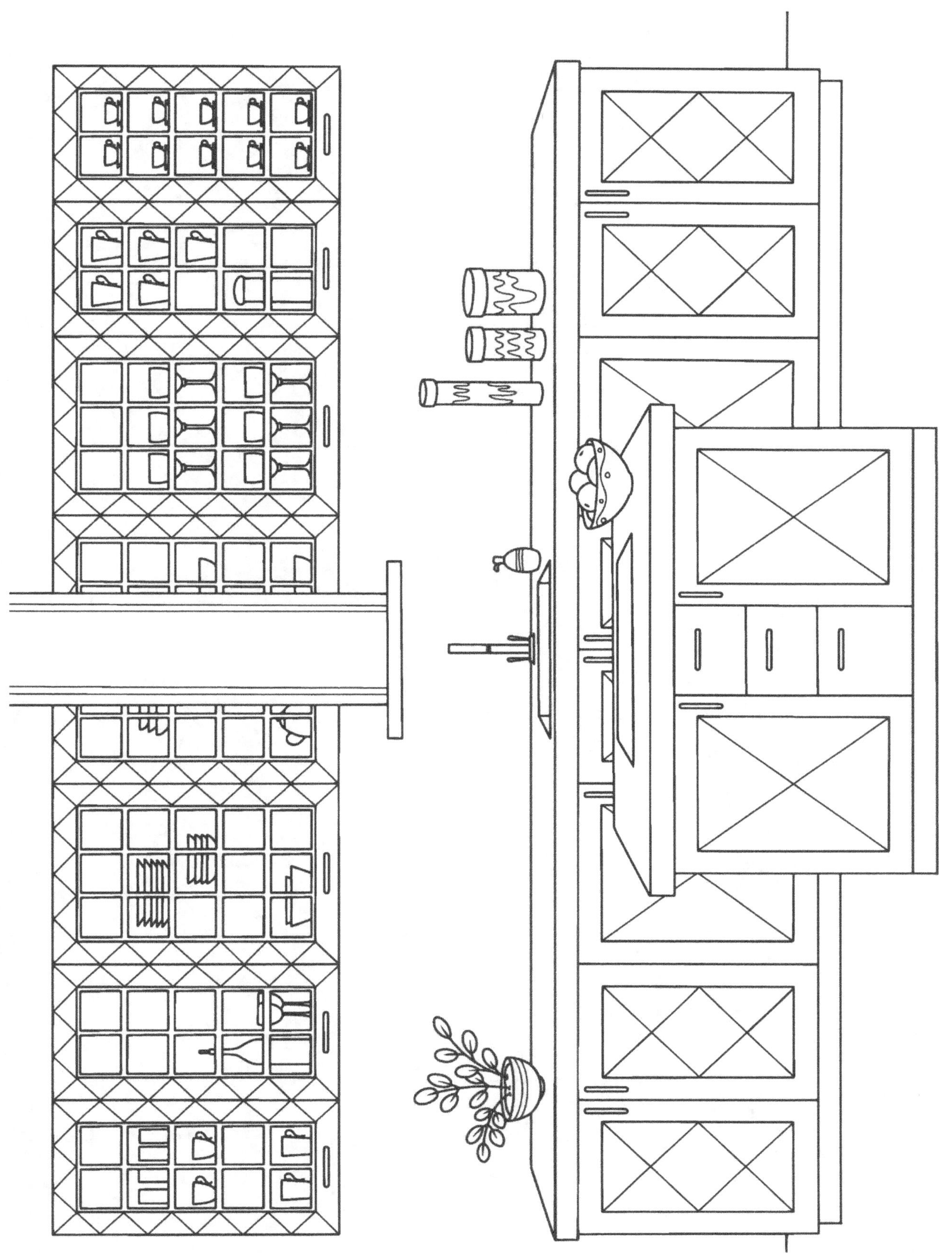

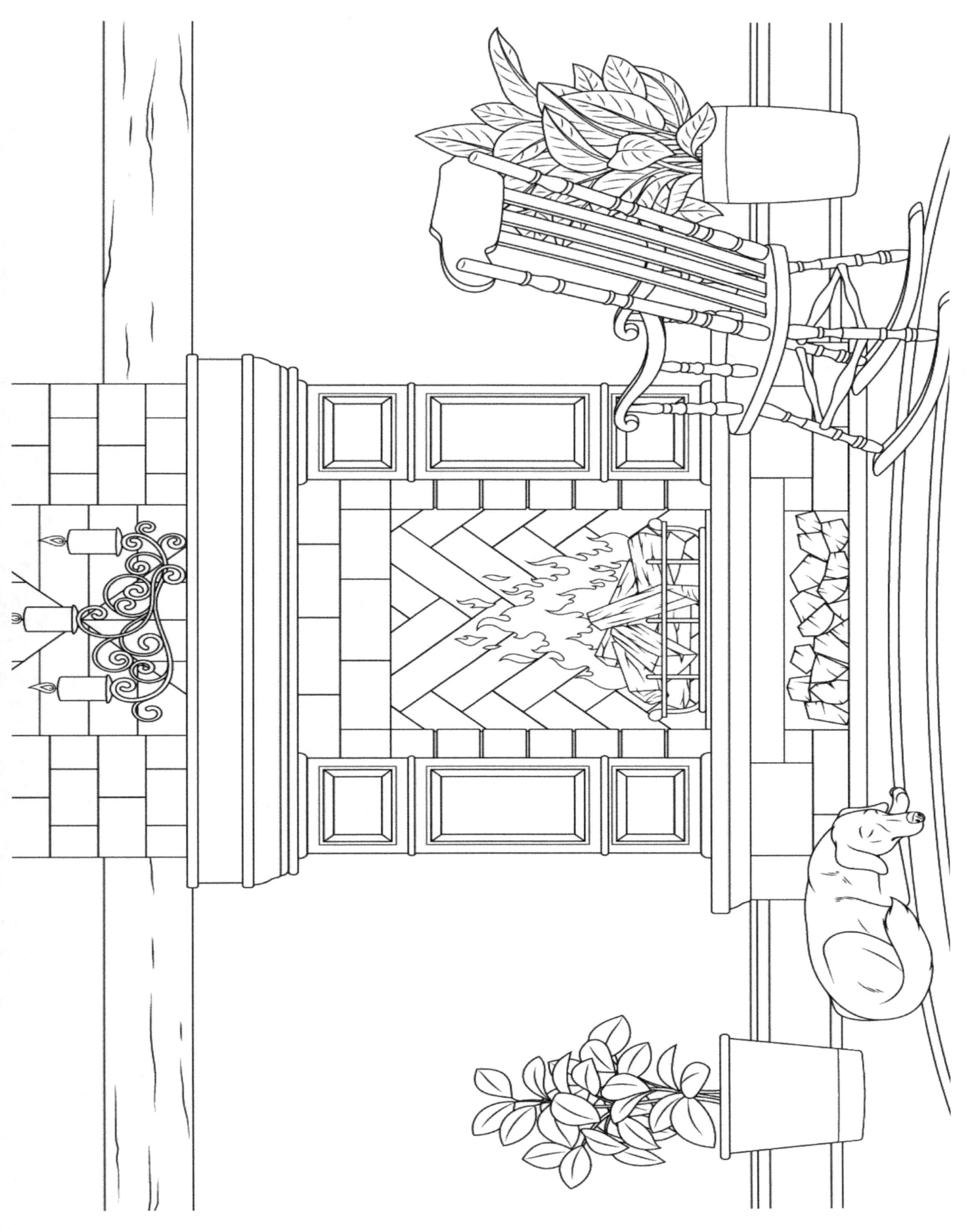

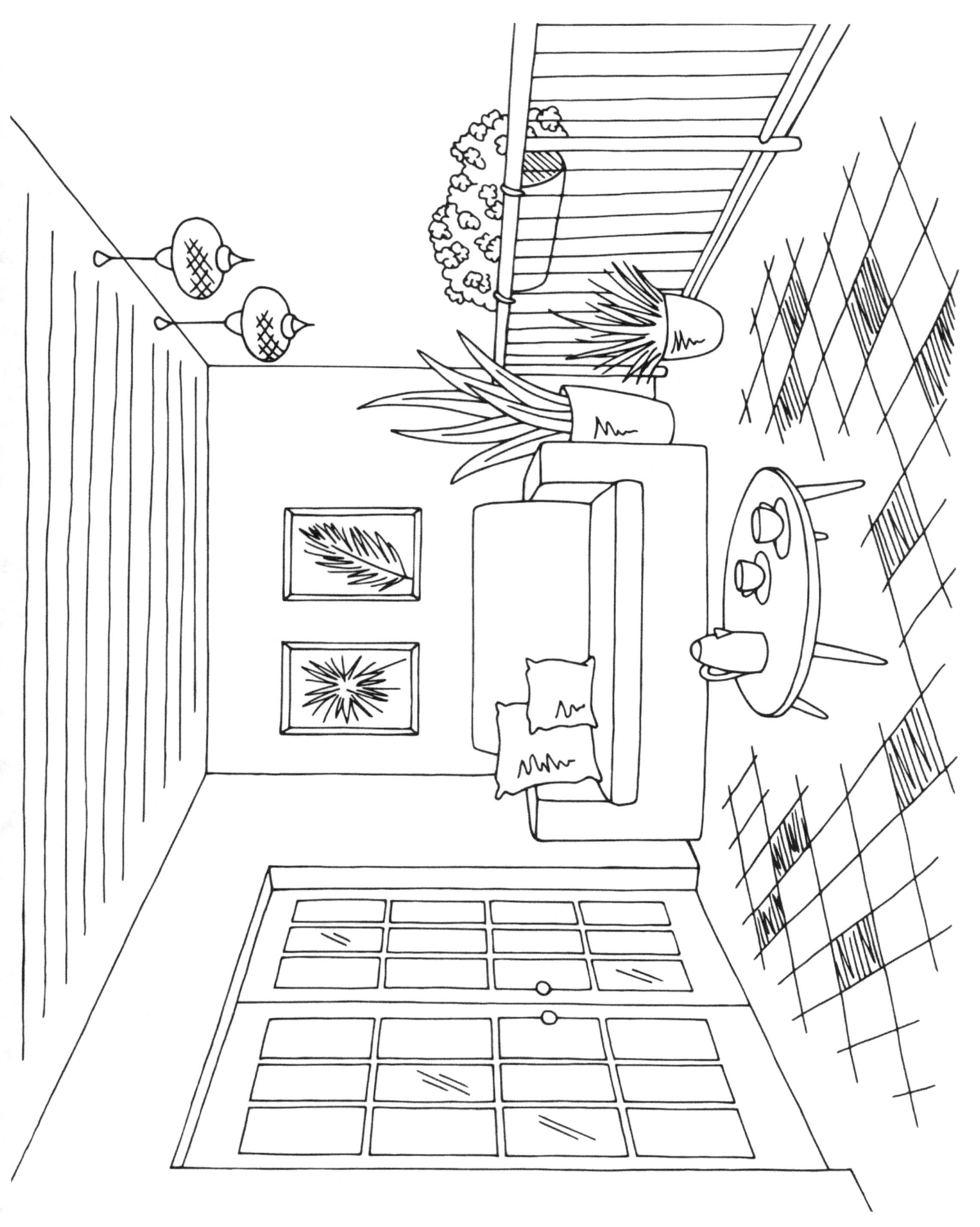

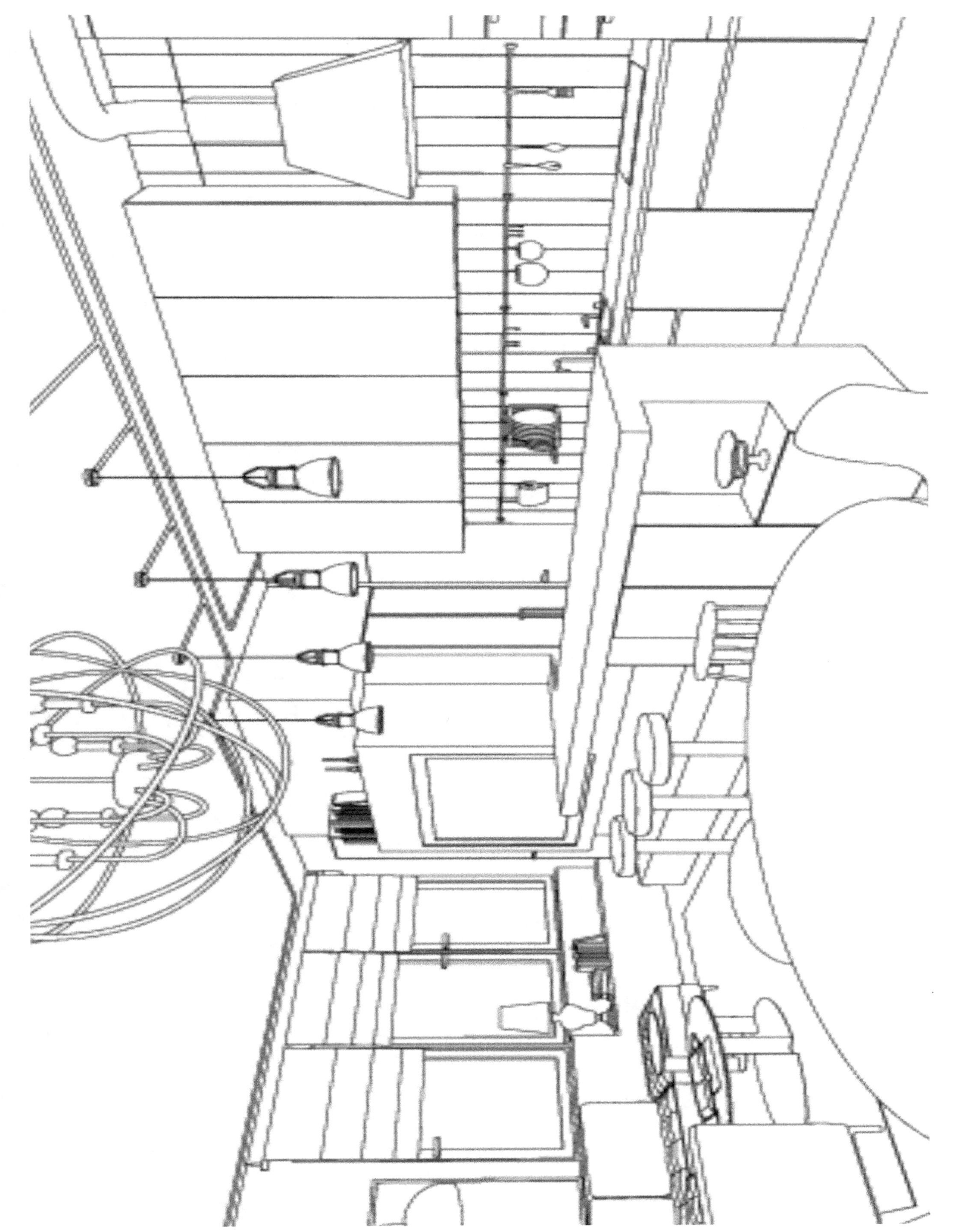

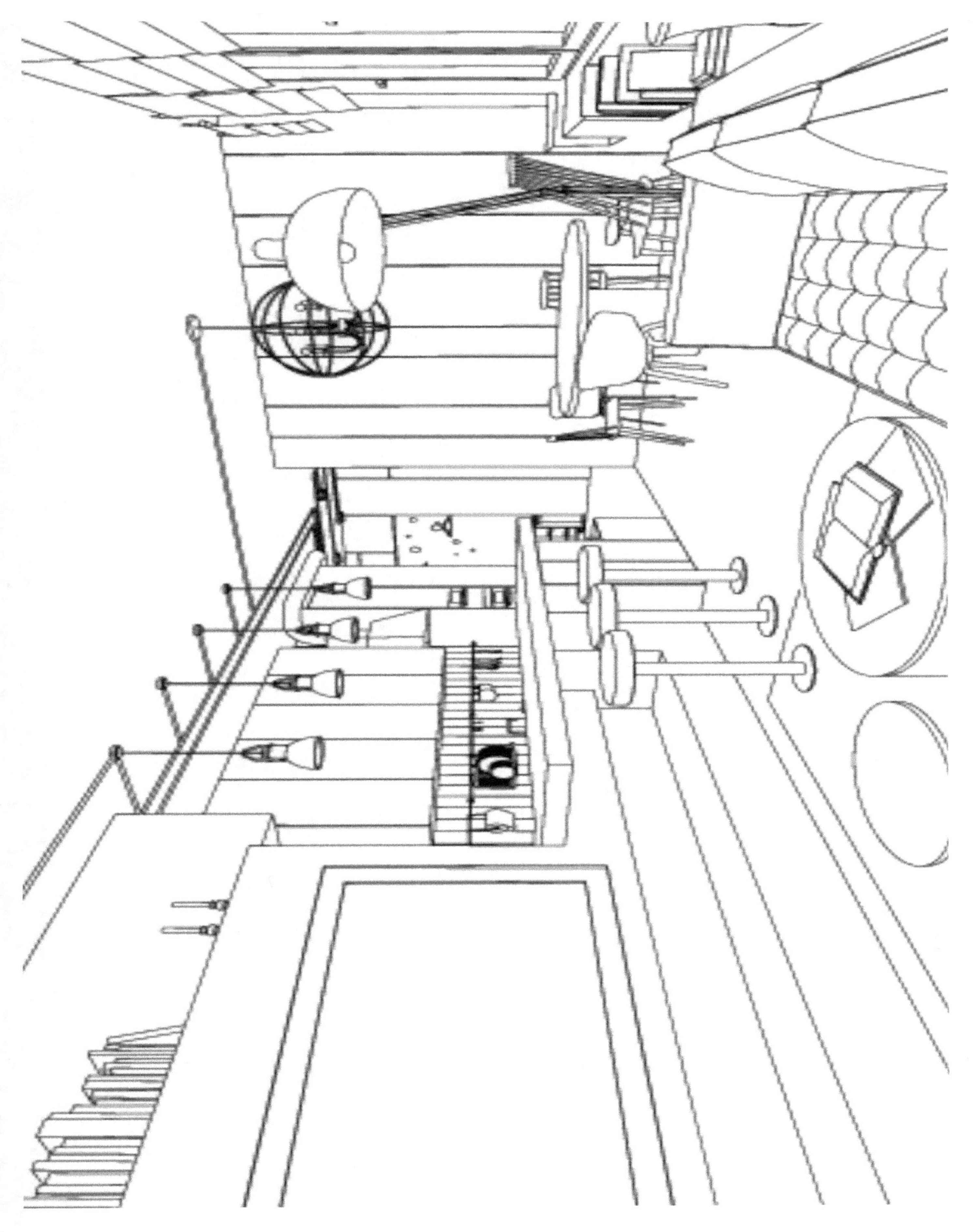

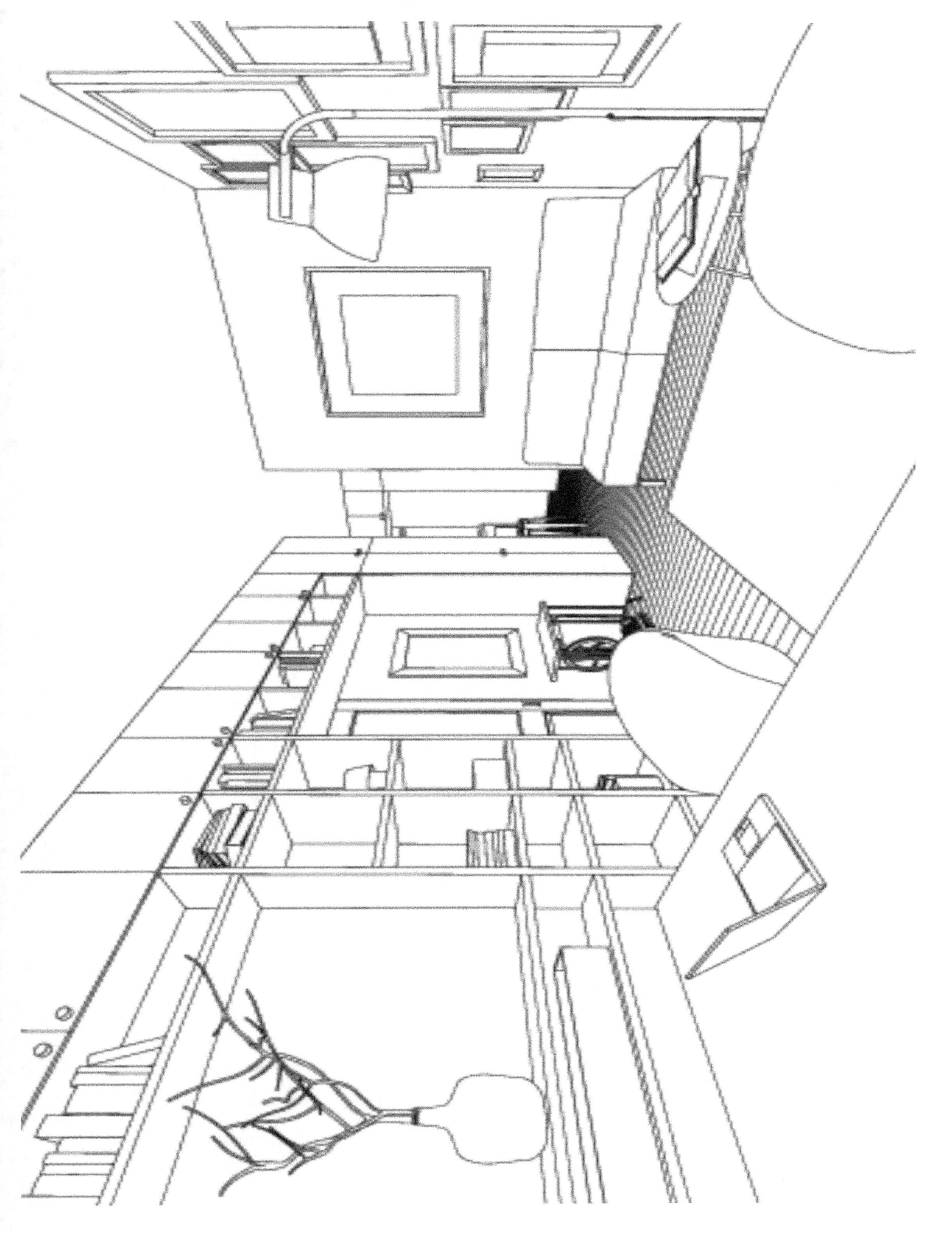

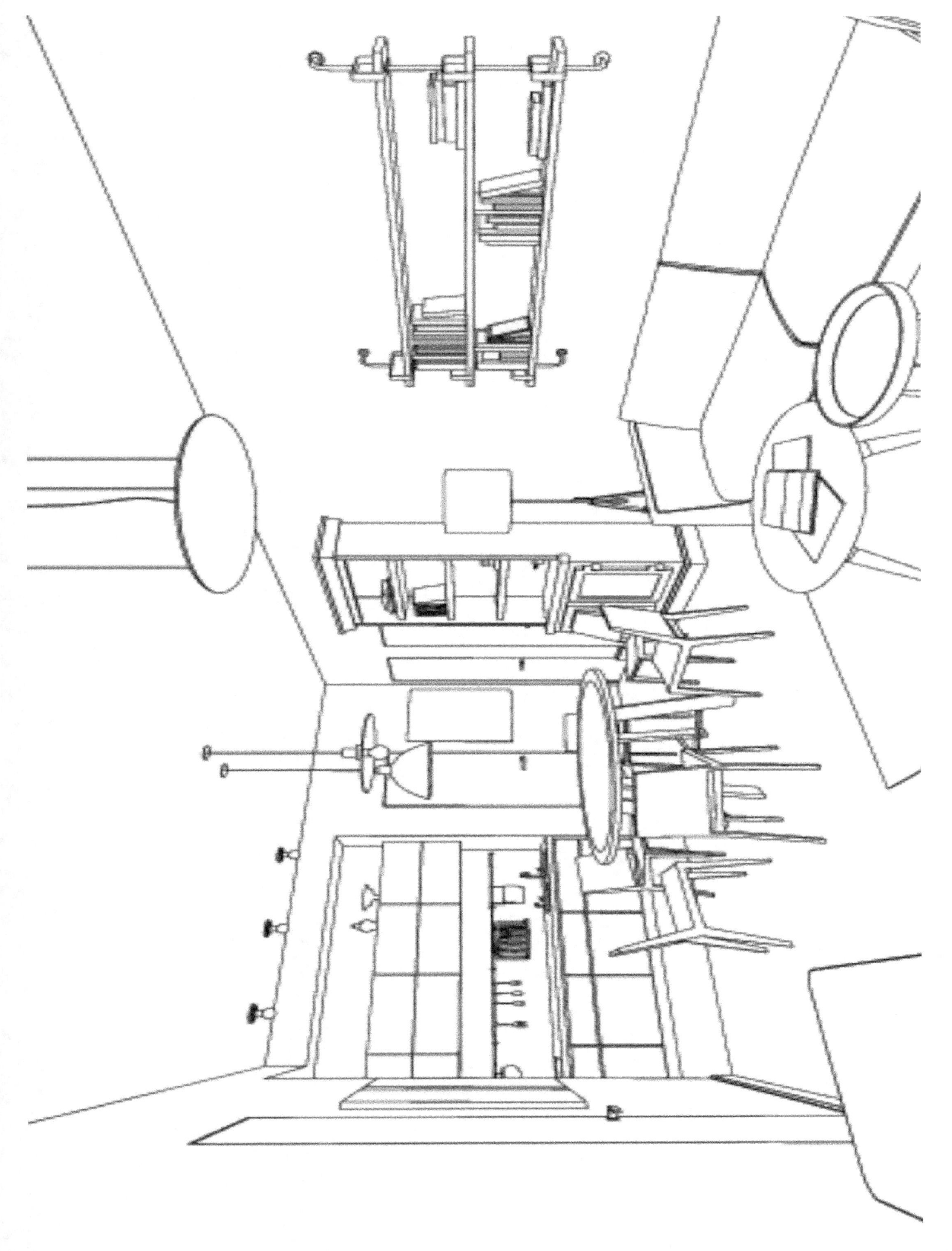

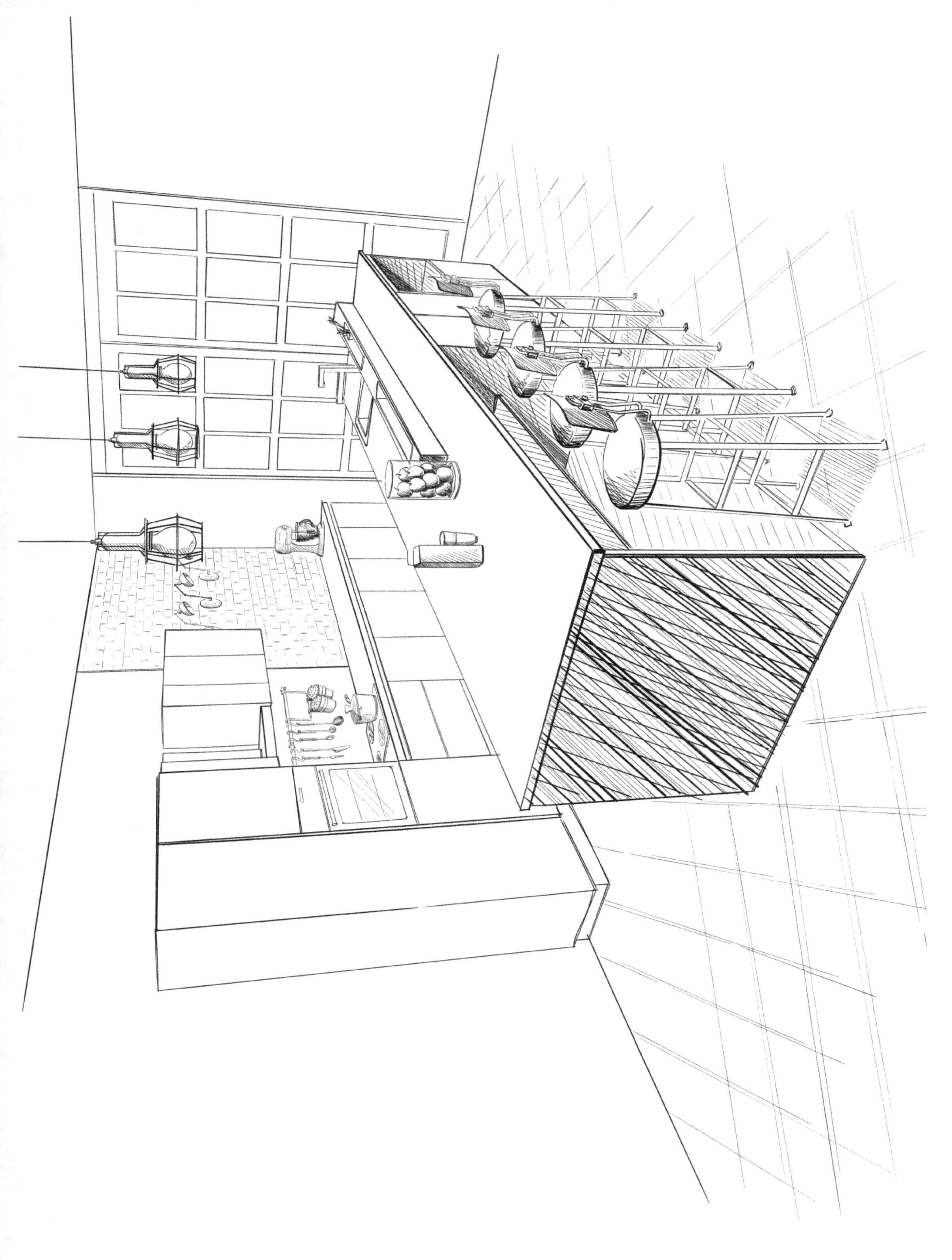

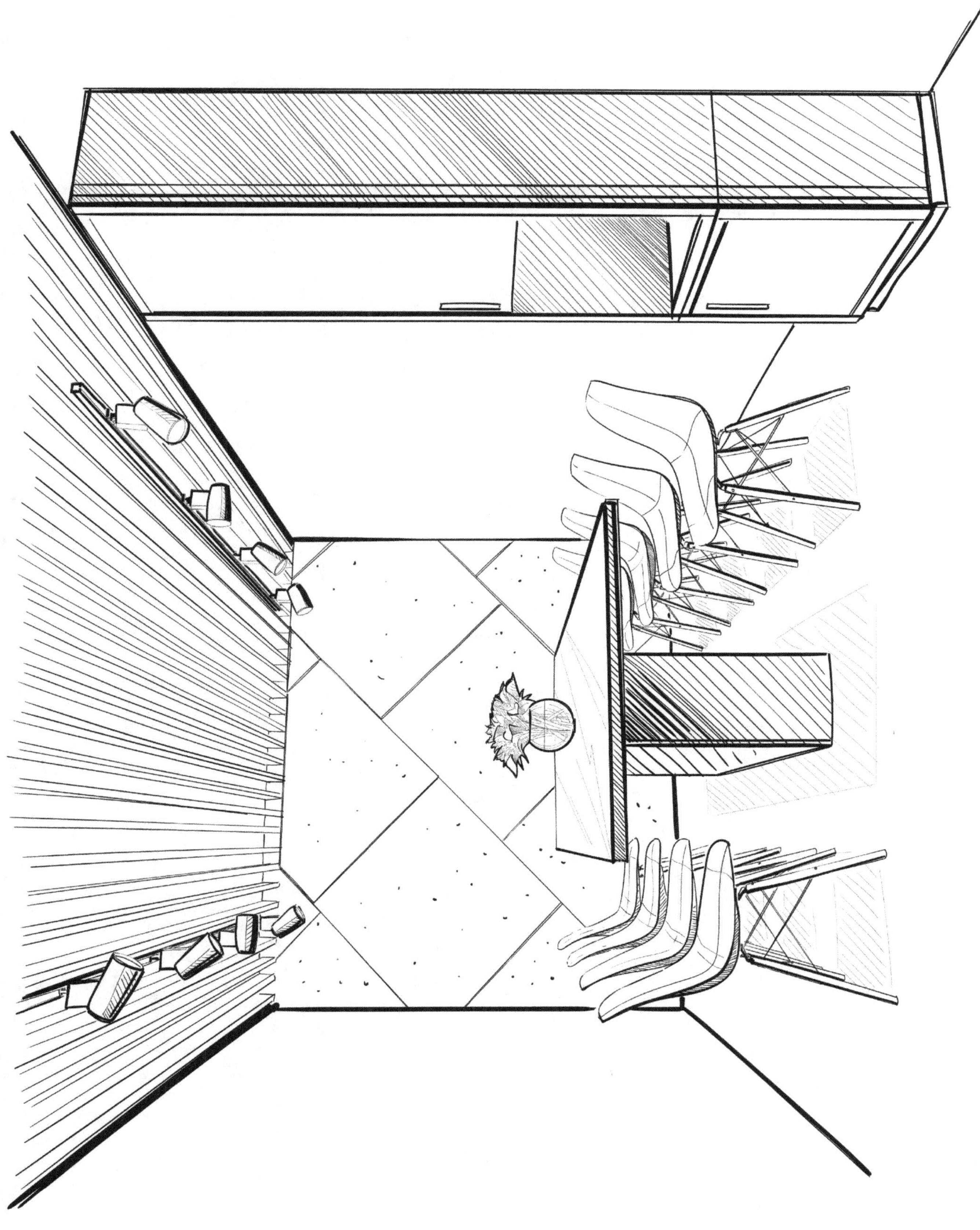